The Anti-racist

Learn the Skills and Methods of Eliminate Racial Prejudice and Discrimination.

Bryce Barhorst

express consent of the Publisher is provided beforehand. Any additional rights reserved.

Furthermore, the information that can be found within the pages described forthwith shall be considered both accurate and truthful when it comes to the recounting of facts.

As such, any use, correct or incorrect, of the provided information will render the Publisher free of responsibility as to the actions taken outside of their direct purview. Regardless, there are zero scenarios where the original author or the Publisher can be deemed liable in any fashion for any damages or hardships that may result from any of the information discussed herein.

Additionally, the information in the following pages is intended only for informational purposes and should thus be thought of as universal. As befitting its nature, it is presented without assurance regarding its prolonged validity or interim quality. Trademarks that are mentioned are done without written consent and can in no way be considered an endorsement from the trademark holder.

Table of Contents

Introduction

It is tough for all of us to believe we should be treated equally while we are all different. The negative differences are considered natural, and the difference is correlated with the so-called lower or higher, or the harmful. It seems ordinary. It is not normal, however. We know something and can then unlearn it. It is tough to accept that not all people are treated equally just because some of us are different. Differences are natural, but some are considered negative and thought of as "lesser" or even "harmful". It seems logical to expect equality, but history has shown it is not. It seems that we must unlearn a lot of the things we know in order to grow.

This book deals with the significance that we assign to inequalities, because of gender, ethnicity and nationality, and their negative impact on the quality of life of millions of people throughout the world. The book also deals with the ongoing struggle to recognize and eventually eradicate prejudice, racial discrimination, and xenophobia from our society as ethical entities. This book is intended as a complete guide for this war.

We have wined and dined in our ignorance enough. We have ended each other's lives over aspects of our lives that do not count. This is the great call to repentance. It is time to regain our sanity. It is time to understand that the ways we have been seeing each other have been misconstrued, and they need to be appropriately amended.

This book also deals with the educated fight against racism. This is not just a book but a call. A call to end racism around the world. A call to stop prejudice. A call to eradicate inhumanity and welcome humanity. A call to end assumptions arrived at based on the disparity in the color of our skins. Let us dive in and end racism together. Happy reading.

Chapter 1: What is Racism?

Racism is a doctrine that fosters privilege, discrimination, hatred, intolerance, criminalization, and extermination. It is institutionalized in government, religions, educational systems, social organizations and media to maintain white supremacy through oppression, subjugation, enslavement, and murder. Much of the institutionalization is covert and unconscious. Most people do not recognize its perpetuation or their participation, but it is there, nonetheless.

Some people confuse prejudice and discrimination with racism, but there is a distinct difference. Prejudice is a dislike, usually negative. Discrimination is an action or unfair treatment. Racism includes both. However, racism has the power to oppress. That power to control a group of people is the difference.

People who are oppressed may be prejudiced or even have the ability to discriminate, but they lack the power to oppress. Ask yourself, "What power do African Americans have, to oppress white folk in the United States?" There is none.

White people have the power to control the image, story and beliefs of African Americans. White people have the power to control jobs/employment, housing, insurance, education, and medical treatment of African Americans. White people control the entire quality of life and death of African Americans—from security and self-respect to purpose/fulfillment. That is the power of racism.

Chapter 2: How to Deal with Racism

Prejudice and dogmatism are lamentably prevalent in this world, and numerous individuals need to confront this miserable reality.

A lot of migrants feel that in their new nation they have lost their certainty; they feel discouraged and lost. In their nation of origin, they were happy and fruitful with plenty of friends and great jobs.

After arriving to their new nation and being confronted with bigotry they find it difficult to prevail in their vocation or even to be acknowledge as professionals. They also experience hatred and a negative energy towards them.

Bigotry is not just about race or religion; it very well can be about sexual inclination or religion. It is about being dismissed for who you are in any capacity.

The best approach to managing bigotry is to initially acknowledge that each individual has the 'opportunity of decision' and has the option to think any way they need. This implies each individual has the option to be a bigot, just as you have the option to practice your religion or seek a new nation to live in.

Now try to understand "opportunity of decision" through the fact that decisions are dependent on training. That is influenced by the fortunate or unfortunate instructions you have been given, misguided judgments or the impact of media narratives.

Plainly, people have a group mindset and think what they are advised to think, without utilizing their individual experiences or sound judgment. Even when their opinion is as unmitigatedly inept, individuals are allowed to follow these bigoted and hurtful narratives. People are just like all other creatures. When you beat them on enough occasions with a stick, they can become frightened when they simply observe a stick. In the same manner, when they hear biased proclamations regularly enough, they will accept what they hear, paying little heed to the fact they can be absolutely unwarranted.

Therefore, like any creature, their decisions, and preferences, are put into their brain, as opposed to create with a target reason or intelligence. Racists can, along these lines, be felt sorry for, as casualties of mental control.

The most significant point to remember is that you are not God. You reserve no option to mention to someone what to think or accept. Similarly, you demand that no one should mention to you what to think and accept. This implies that you can have faith in one religion and do not need anybody advising you to follow an alternate one. At that point, you reserve no option to tell that individual that they ought not to think your religion is awful. Everybody can think about what they need, it is quite reasonable.

Give them the opportunity to have their bigoted and preferential perspectives, since you request the option to not be a supremacist. You have the opportunity to not think and feel pessimistic towards someone, by the shade of their skin or some other inclination. We do not reserve the option to pick something we need, when we do not give others that equivalent right.

Furthermore, this is one way to be safe from prejudice. When a bigoted individual puts you down, and you realize that the affront or the reason for their antagonistic view towards you is absolutely bogus and illegitimate, you will not get injured or insulted in any capacity.

As a five-year-old, a remark about your physical appearance may not influence you, since you are just a few years old; similarly, an older individual can be just as uninformed.

At the point when you are confronted with any bigotry or preferences against you in any capacity whatsoever, you can allow them the option to be that way and not complain at all That way you will display such a quality of character, which does not disintegrate under their assault and disdain.

This quality will hopefully show them that their preference is not legitimate, and that in spite of their assaults, you can stay cool and solid, and not fight back. Your distinction is unmistakably better than them. In this way you may change their view and possibly open up their psyche, so they are not bigoted.

It might be just a simple procedure, yet it is one that will stop you from feeling awful, and in any event, it is also an opportunity to change the world one person at a time.

We have a complete list of observations regarding racism that make us feel that it is very difficult to even think about it. It is difficult to talk about racism, because human nature is totally involved in it.

Here are some ways all of us (most often white groups) grip onto racism. The first option might be long, but it needs to be dealt with in the right way. Be assured the next four will be much more friendly.

Identify Racial Imbalances and Differences.

Racism yields racial imbalances and aberrations in each segment of private and open life. That is true for legislative issues, human services, criminal equity, instructions, salaries, work, and home possessions. Being antiracist implies finding out about and recognizing imbalances and aberrations that give white individuals or any other race, material focal points over non-white individuals. So, a racist examination showcases poor, and more regrettable results for dark-skinned Americans and clarifies that the issue is not the people, but the approaches that put certain groups at an unmistakable drawback.

Confront the Racist Thoughts You Have Held or Keep Holding Onto.

When you start distinguishing racial differences, you need to look at whether your own perspectives, convictions, or voting preferences have legitimized racial disparity.

In case you are that parent who will not send your child to a predominantly, dark-skinned school, consider how that decision is impacted by your perspective on discipline, approaches to contract schools, and other arrangements that are profoundly interwoven with race and racism. Do you vote in favor of the educational committee or the city council candidates, who would prefer not to address instructive aberrations or neutralize supporters attempting to increment instructive value? Do you realize that subsidizing arrangements influence how assets are allotted to schools, and why those practices can create racial variations?

Understand How Your Antiracism Should Be Intersectional

A strategy that creates disparity among white and Native American individuals, yields imbalances between white men and Native American ladies. If one accepts that dark-skinned men are better than dark-skinned ladies, then that individual will not have the option to perceive how certain thoughts and strategies negatively influence dark-skinned ladies in our communities. Since race converges with various other parts of an individuals' being, including their sex, class, and ethnicity, it is natural to utilize an intersectional approach while being antiracist.

Understand the Meaning of Racist

Discussions about racism regularly happen when members cannot characterize the importance of the word. Merriam-Webster defines racism as "a conviction that race is the essential determinant of human attributes and limits, and that racial differences produce an inalienable prevalence of a specific race." Few individuals would concede that definition mirrors their perspectives; yet all things considered, they deliberately or accidentally, believe in or hold on to racist thoughts all the time.

Stop Saying "I Am Not Racist"

In case you are a white liberal who sees yourself as not racist, you still may not send your kid to a nearby government funded school, due to the fact that the populace is primarily African American. That decision is racist. The antiracist position would be to consider enrolling your kid, or even finding out about the disparities influencing that school, so as to fight them.

Not Agreeing on Racism:

Most of us do not actually know what racism is. If we look at the exact definition of racial discrimination in a dictionary, we will, of course, get a practically sound explanation. Racism is discrimination based on contest which decides the superiority of one over another.

Yes, this is not enough. Think of all those ideas and events which you have constantly heard regarding the issue of racism. Do you find that this definition has captured them all?

Now, if we go to another search engine, like Wikipedia, we will get more solid definitions; however, they follow the same path as the aforementioned definitions. After using more than seventy odd words to explain the meaning of racism, the website proceeds to inform us on how 'notorious' the meaning of racism can be, as no one will support this definition. Neither the scholars nor the parents, and not even other allies like the racists.

Based on all the things we have practiced like a black person and on top of all the things we have understood, processed, considered, or debated over many years, racism is the problem. It is that we and most of the people, do not subscribe to such description of racial discrimination which allows for this issue to continue. So, we need to explain it differently.

Racism or racial discrimination is an institutionalized structure intended to make patterns of unfairness based on race. Though the words are mine, although it is not a unique description, many antiracist thinkers, have been utilizing comparable definitions for years. While we mention some new words, we are also required to define them. This is a requirement that we will accomplish before we are all done with this book.

Prejudice is the predetermined belief of a human being that has no basis on reality or real knowledge and focuses only on the label. Anybody can be prejudiced.

Inequity is one of the acts that has its base on prejudice. The superlative used to explain the conditions in which any person either punishes or else discards the progression of other human beings based on prejudice. This is again something anybody could do.

Black or white supremacy: People who are either black or white, who have similar ancestry, develop into two totally dissimilar cultures. White people have a particular faith in their whiteness and the fact that white people are naturally superior. Black people have the same view of being dark-skinned.

Both of them are extremely detailed strains of discrimination. Racism or racial discrimination, though, stresses that this tree develops from white ascendancy, and mechanically starts to produce the mechanisms of racial discrimination. On the other side, the small bonsai plant that comes from the black ascendancy is hardly noticeable.

White People Do Not Think They are Bad

The dilemma we have been exploring so far is that white people do not want to listen to a description of racism that makes them look bad. They do not like to pay attention to unfair standards or structures of beauty, and to communally constructed inferiority complexes, or to how there is consistent racial profiling. To use such effects to describe racial discrimination would in fact be immoral. We are believed to follow the hundred years old tradition of racial discrimination that accepted all the aforementioned examples as normal. Of course, they don't need to recognize how significant race is to the definition made by them, because they do not need have to consider it. The world around us reinforces their existence and self-importance all the time. They do not understand how it is based on racial discrimination because it is normal to them.

The previously mentioned explanation also touches upon the matter of privileges given to whites, specifically, that drives them crazy. White people do not appreciate how, if they are unemployed or poor, they are still advantaged. We have many articles which explore this fact and if we the Black people are here, we most likely had to fight tooth and nail to reach here. One frequently seen example is how if we take one homeless white person and clean that person up, the guy will most probably receive a job offer easier than a capable black person. It is not bad to have privilege, though when we describe dispensation as monetary, we dismiss a complete list of perks or advantages that the white guys always receive from racial discrimination and it does not matter what amount of that money they keep in their pocket.

If we are white and we come to a decision that we are not going to discuss about the idea of race any longer, and the world lets this happen, we are privileged. There is no black person in the world who would ignore the racial discrimination issue. White guys could ignore from the issue at any given point and it has zero repercussions on the lives. Even the rich black groups would not do the same.

Spending Time on Giving Coverage

. We should not be fighting with the individuals; we should keep fighting with the machine that uses part of the community as cannon fodder for the smaller portion of the community it intends to help.

Giving Credit to Systems Other Than Racism:

Sometimes people disregard racial discrimination as an actual issue and focus more on the two-party system, greed and classism as though they are on a similar level as racism. If we somehow fix classism, would that be able to end racism? Or, if we find a better way to secure jobs, food and housing to every person who asked, at a level which has made them indisputably content, would racial discrimination still not exist? No doubt it will never change. People perform racist activities even if they do not have that stuff. It is why we as black people, when we are walking down the street and notice a white guy without a roof over his head living on street, put forward a dollar. And he would still call us a 'black' or 'nigger'. He might be a sufferer of greed and classism, though even if we offer him a good job and an attractive house, gift him all his teeth back and everything else he could think of, he would still not change himself and have to suffer from racial discrimination. Sometimes, these guys become super villains in terms of racism. The calculation works for all the big problems we face, such as getting rid of two-party structure and we are still left with racial discrimination. We find a way to put, real people into power as a tainted view of kindness. That is what we are all eventually asking for. We can also figure out a way to create a system which can fight issues on the stage that social/cultural/political structures control. Then all the other useless things will be consumed for the sake of a society, which not only enjoys their differences by celebrating them, but also actually embraces that these differences will not be tolerated in the future.

Let us be clear that this is not a competition or a challenge. No one is going to take part in a movie like *Hunger Games*. We do not take joy in becoming a former slave, existing as a result of a battle in the racial discrimination environment. We point out these angles, because the views can transform the worth of some undervalued issues. We discuss race. These points target the cause of our troubles, the resource code, and the energy that helps the engine keep all other problems in existence.

Our Feelings First

Most of the time, we wish to call out one of our friends for saying something that has hurt us; however, we are scared of hurting them back and injuring their feelings. It is obvious, but do not forget that you too are hurt. You are the person who has been offended initially, and you are the person who has been betrayed, and you have let your friend's remark influence you. It is completely your right to talk about it. You should say that you are feeling uncomfortable and explain that first to your friend.

Ask a Racist to Explain What He Means

When somebody makes a racist remark, we should ask them to clearly explain themselves. By saying, please explain, this could force them to consider what they have said, and for sure they will realize that they have said something incorrect.

Do Not Be Scared to Discuss

Sometimes, behaving like a smart person proves to be the greatest method for proving to someone that they have actually screwed up. If you think that something is not right, you should say something back mockingly. You will use this as a method of calling out your pal. Please do not rely only on this, though. You need to showcase your talent by dropping some humor at the same time.

Call out

Doing this can scary but sometimes it is needed. Starting such debates in a group, specifically for very sensitive matters like racism, is not so comfortable. Your heart may start pounding and your tongue may get stuck; but it is good to casually bring up something that made you very uncomfortable.

Friends will listen

Real and genuine friends treat us with respect. Sharing your thoughts with your friends is good. Your friends will understand the feelings behind the expression. However, if they continue to repeat it then those people do not respect you, and they are not genuine and real friends.

Keep Distance

If after repeatedly expressing your unhappiness you continue to face the same behavior, it is better to ignore them. If they are again spouting off slurs for laughs, then you need to maintain your distance. It is difficult but accept the fact that they do not actually respect you. The friendship is poisonous and needs to end. Keep in mind that you deserve something better than that. We have some ways to handle racist behavior in our community. Let us see some of them.

- **Reacting calmly to the situation.** Do not overreact. Everything has a solution. Reacting in anger may cause some not only physical but emotional damage as well. It also affects your mental health. Do not forget that anger is not always helpful.

- **Convey discomfort or disapproval.** Without becoming frustrated, take a defensive reaction.

- **Question the usage of action or words** so that you can measure their intent.

- **Convey the feelings.** Let the people around you know how that joke or comment makes you feel uncomfortable.

- **Question the fear**. Asking for someone's fear could be very valuable moments to inquire about somebody's ignorance and fear.

- **Do not get triggered.** Racists always try to push your buttons to make you angry. So, keep walking.

- **Compliment** them on something.

Studies have found that standing up for yourself is good. It will satisfy you, that you at least did something good for the sufferer of that racist, and it is probably better for the assaulter. Racists often think that they have more support from the society. If they are not stopped, they will continue to think and behave in the same way.

We can respond to them by creating a safe distance from them, because they do not agree with our views. We should in fact wish them the best with their lives and let them know that the moment they adjust their tone, they are allowed to re-enter your life by apologizing. Let them know that God created us because he loves all colors.

Ignore the Original Emotional Reaction.

No anger: If you do not control your anger, you will end up suffering from high blood pressure and stress.

Racists are learners: There is a possibility that they may be less open-minded and understanding, compared to you. They may not know that the comments or actions made by them are racist.

Ignorance: Sometimes, they ignore you to prove that they are not racist, a natural behavior. In fact, we can use humor and wit to defeat them.

Secure the personal details: Racists always try to know your personal details to hurt you even more strongly. Do not reveal these details to others. They love to know your details to use the information against you in the future.

Save energy: To get attention, racists make comments which hurt people. They feel happy the moment they receive a response from you.

Focus: Focusing on other things is a good way to ignore the racists.

No teaching: Do not involve yourself into arguments and try to teach them about racism.

No preaching: Until you see some indication that the person is eager to pay attention, and is open to having a conversation, you should not try to alter his or her beliefs.

If you are content in your skin and witness a racist act, we can try to apply these strategies. If a person abuses you verbally, publish the story in the newspaper and see the effect it has.

There are many open colleges that offer books, blogs and articles to help us prevent racist attacks and bullying. The articles and books include the various methods of bullying, and discuss ways to handle them physically and mentally. These books specifically focus on teachers and children.

Chapter 3: The Superiority and Inferiority Concept

Racism is not just a black-and white race issue, because in every society on the face of the earth, there are two major groups of people: those who feel they are superior, and those who have been forcefully made to feel that they are inferior. This superiority is driven by fear and greed. There is never any justification for taking advantage of other people, but for this to happen, people must be reduced to something less than they actually are. **When people have been bombarded with a lie for a long time, they believe it.** People will keep living this lie because their subconscious minds have been programmed by this faulty information. The subconscious mind will not distinguish between what is true and what is false. The subconscious mind believes whatever information is fed into it and will use that information to determine the action each individual take.

While racism has been amplified in societies like the United States of America, where the arbitrary white/black divide has heightened this issue, we should not be distracted by the severity of this problem. Unfortunately, many have cast racism as something that exists strictly between the white and black races. This way of looking at the issue has not helped us solve the problem. It is high time that we try a new approach.

If there is only one human race, then the term racism needs to be redefined or discarded altogether.

Therefore, instead of isolating and treating the manifestation of ethnocentrism 'gone wild' that exists between the white and black races, we should be looking at interactions within the entire human race, because this broad division between white and black is artificial and unfounded.

Remember that these two brothers had never heard of racism and had no socio-economic division or class distinction whatsoever. This did not prevent anger, fear, envy, and jealousy from driving one of them to murder the other. Therefore, it will be naïve to invoke racism to be the root cause of what happened here. It seems there is something deeper at play here. When we dig a little deeper, we find out that the parents of these two brothers were living in a state of perfection, until their disobedience brought in sin, death, and destruction.

From that point till now, the human race has had a difficult time relating and living in harmony with one another, because humankind is out of harmony with the Creator. Although we can easily get distracted by the so-called manifestation of racism, the issue is deeper than that. I have already established that race is a social construct, and it is not real. It is some sort of a camouflage that is used to cover up a deeper and more serious problem.

An Issue of the Heart

Whatever causes people to hate, discriminate, and at times, murder others, is an issue of the heart. We have already mentioned that the heart of a man is desperately wicked. Out of a wicked heart flow all sorts of evil things, so the heart is where we need to focus our efforts when trying to address the issue of racism. A desperately wicked human heart needs deliverance. There is no way the amount of melanin in somebody's skin will justify enslaving, mistreating, or taking advantage of them.

You may be saying that racism is real because of the historical records of enslavement of people from Africa, the lynching in southern US, segregation, Jim Crow and the civil rights movement, and much more. This is just part of the picture and a manifestation of a deeper problem. The Africans, that ended up in chains in the US and their descendants, were subjected to all sorts of inhumane treatment. They were originally caught and sold by fellow Africans. This point is being raised here not to blame or castigate anybody, but to point out the depravity in every human heart, and to underscore the fact that given the right circumstances, all humans, no matter their skin color, are capable of committing terrible acts against other humans.

Therefore, instead of focusing on racism, which is just a symptom of a sick, desperately wicked human heart, we should be looking at the heart. Take for example, the terrible events that led to the Holocaust and the death of six million Jews. Did this barbaric act have anything to do with skin color, or was it driven by the evil in the hearts of the perpetrators, who raised bogeymen, in the name of the master race, to justify slaughtering millions of people?

We must peel back this camouflage, and get to the evil in the hearts of people that is manifested through acts of violence, hate, discrimination, etc.

We are back to where we started. These things that come out of the heart are bad, and nobody wants them or likes them. For example, when a police officer guns down an unarmed black male, there is outrage and cries of racism. The reasoning is that, the likes of Michael Brown were shot because of their skin color, but the reason may be deeper than the fact that the police officer is white and the victim black. According to Jesus Christ, there is something more sinister at work here, and it is the state of the heart. Everything that happens on the outside is a result of what is happening on the inside.

In other words, if a person does not have hate, murder, or evil thoughts in their hearts, there is no way they will allow the color of somebody's skin to prompt them to shoot indiscriminately. While some may argue that it is a "chicken and egg" situation, I will argue that external factors reveal the true intent of the heart. If the heart is not wicked and evil, it will not become evil overnight.

Refusing that sin does not exist and wishing it to go away has not helped at all. People, by default, are not good, and out of them come deeds that are harmful to other people. The manifestation of racism is a direct result of sin. In other words, racism is a symptom of sin that plagues all mankind.

There is no society on earth in which you will not find the manifestation of issues of the heart: evil thoughts, murder, adultery, sexual immorality, theft, false testimony, slander, fear, greed, hate, etc. all are present. We are aware that when we say somebody is a racist, it is because the person has manifested one or more of these issues of the heart. These issues of the heart have a serious negative impact on other people when expressed by those we consider racist. If racism had no adverse effect on people, it would not be a problem at all. However, we know that racism has the potential of destroying lives, and at times it literally does that.

We have clearly seen that racism is just a smoke screen. It is masking a more serious problem, which is the sin in the hearts of people. To resolve the problem of racism, sin has to be identified and dealt with. If we continue to ignore sin and try to legislate the problem, we will continue to get limited success, because we are just adding a band-aid to a deep and inflected wound. Now is the time to make some changes and get to the root of the problem of racism. There is no point in focusing on the symptoms because it is not delivering the outcome that we desire and need.

Hurting People Hurt Others

The human race is hurting because of the disobedience of Adam and Eve. The original harmony that was disrupted in the beginning has been replaced by death, sickness, and decay.

We all know that racism is bad because of the negative impact it has on other people. But the question is, why do people hate, discriminate, and treat other people wrong? Why does somebody need to feel that they are superior to others? In short, why cannot all of us just get along? How can another human being think that others are subhuman because of where and of whom gave birth to them?

You can be in a country where the caste system is prevalent, and they may justify it one way or the other, but there is no justification to relegating people to a position of servitude for life. Any system that imposes limitations on who goes where, who interacts with whom, and who gets married to whom, needs to be re-examined.

Those who need to feel superior over other people are suffering from a superiority complex, and they need to get down from their high horses. Just because somebody thinks they are superior does not necessarily mean that they are superior.

Even if they feel that they are superior, it does not make it true. People deal with their hurt feelings in different ways, and some think that feeling superior over other humans gives them a sense of power and purpose. Nothing can fill the void that is in the heart of each one of us. This is the void that only God can fill. Except throughout human history, people have tried everything under the sun to fill this void to no avail.

If you meet somebody who thinks that another human being is beneath their feet, and they are ready to discredit them because of the amount of melanin in their skin, you should pity that person because they are hurting badly and need healing. There is not one iota of data that supports some of the absurd ideas about the human race that are perpetuated across the globe.

When you take a closer look at how people interact with each other, you will realize that ignorance and misinformation are driving most of the beliefs and attitudes people have towards each other.

Every country in the world is hurting people. The entire world is filled with people that hurt people, and these hurting people are hurting other people. To reduce this monstrous human problem to racism is trivializing this issue. Ever since people started blaming racism as the cause of the hate, anger, mistreatment, and even murder, the issue of racism has not been resolved. Instead, racism is on the rise, and the definition has morphed into something entirely different, depending on where you are.

Lately, there have been talks of racism on the rise in Europe because of the influx of immigrants from other parts of the world. Again, the news media adore sensational headlines, and focuses on the symptoms rather than the root cause. The symptoms make good viewership but does not necessarily try to resolve the problem.

Fear is a stronger emotion than racism, and fear is usually driven by ignorance. Ignorance here is used not as an insulting term, but to explain a lack of information. When you have an influx of people into an area with customs, beliefs and other ways of doing things that are very different from those of the people in their new environment, there is bound to be some distress on both sides.

On the one hand, those that feel their space is being invaded will try to push back because they are afraid that their way of life is being threatened. In addition to the fear of losing their way of life, there is the fear of limited resources, jobs, and depressing wages. The other big fear is an increase in crime.

These fears are not limited to Europe or North America alone. These reactions are common among people all over the world. Every time people move into an area, other people may feel threatened and become fearful.

Hurting people indeed hurt others, and this is a universal problem and should not be reduced to a white-and-black race problem. While there are different degrees of the manifestation of this problem, the underlying characteristics of hate, discrimination, mistreatment, and murder have cut across every society, culture, and nation.

The Driver of Superiority Complex

It is important for us to understand the phenomena of superiority and inferiority complexes. They have existed in all human societies through the ages. Today, no matter where you go, you will find that society is broadly divided into two main groups: those that think they are superior to others, and those who have been relegated, forced or brainwashed to believe that they are inferior. We may be splitting hairs to get to the intricacies of these phenomena, but each society has different ways of classifying who is superior and who is inferior. In some cases, the amount of money and material possessions you have define your position. In other countries, the social class or caste in which somebody is born in determines if they are considered inferior or superior. The arbitrary criteria used to divide people into these two broad categories are not based on any facts that can be substantiated.

All humans are equal because when all the external and material possessions are stripped, the human spirit is the same. Our true essence is our spirit, and it is a distraction when we focus solely on the body. This is why using skin color to determine somebody's worth is so inhumane, degrading, insulting, and demeaning. It is also why many people are completely opposed to any form of racism, and rightfully so, because it takes away human dignity and reduces people to something they were not created to be. All were created with and endowed with equal rights that should not be usurped by any person, government, or political ideology.

Now, let us take a look at the history and some of the drivers of superiority and inferiority complexes. We will start with a broad look at the interaction of

Europeans with other people (but not because the Europeans are the worst offenders).

When you look at human history, from Egypt, the cradle of civilization, to the Babylonians, Persians, Romans, Byzantines, Mayans, Aztecs and even modern history, you will see some similarities between the conquered and their conquerors. We are not trying to classify who committed the most evil here, or who committed the most egregious crimes against humanity. The purpose of highlighting this interplay of superiority and inferiority complexes is to show that it is a common human problem that has occurred throughout human history and is still alive and well today. Therefore, we should be careful not to pin it on a single group of people. The temptation to do so is extremely strong because what the Europeans did during the last few centuries of human history is still fresh in our minds. We are living with some of those realities today, and it is going to take a while to resolve some of these issues.

Take the case of Africa. In 1884, Europeans gathered in Berlin and portioned the continent between themselves. Each European power grabbing whatever chunk of Africa they considered juicy enough for themselves. They cared little about the impact these arbitrary lines were going to have on the continent. They also did not show any consideration for all the different independent countries that were already existing within these carved-out territories. Some of their arbitrary lines divided different ethnic groups and placed them under different countries where different languages were imposed on them. In some cases, parts of the same kingdom were placed under French rule and others under English rule.

When these territories were colonized and arbitrarily declared as nations, they held the mistaken assumption that these separate independent kingdoms, made of up different ethnicities, will just get along. You do not impose a nation onto people who are not ready, or willing, to be part of a nation. The colonizers had a nonchalant attitude towards these so-called 'primitive' natives: all they had to do was toe the line and do what their 'masters' demanded. After all, the Europeans knew better than the Africans and could impose on them whatever they deemed necessary. To effectively administer these artificially created countries, the colonizers used intimidation, propaganda, subjugation, and distortion of information to strip the colonized of their sense of dignity, self-worth, and purpose.

It is worth noting that colonization was not an act of charity because it was driven by these same issues of the heart. At this point in history, most of the European powers colonized other countries because they were driven partly by the industrial revolution that started in Britain. They needed raw materials for their industries, and they needed markets to sell their finished goods. These European powers were not only interested in trading with these countries, but they wanted to subjugate, occupy, and rule over them.

We are talking about independent countries that were taking good care of their affairs without any outside intervention. You may be wondering how the Europeans succeeded in subduing other countries. Each country used different tactics. The English specialized in indirect rule, while the French mastered direct rule. The common thread is that Europeans figured out a way to present themselves as superior to the people that they met. This behavior, as I already stated, is not unique to the Europeans. The Romans are guilty of it too; the

Arabs and all the major powers that conquered and ruled over other people did it too.

The process of subjugating other people starts with devaluing them, and creating a false image about them, to the point that they believe it and start perpetuating it. The people had to be distracted from what they had, in order for it to be taken away from them or bought at extremely low prices. For example, when you visit many European countries, you see artwork and artifacts that were looted from all over the world. The natives were made to understand that their art was primitive, demonic, and should be discarded. These people happily gave them away, among many other things, to embrace this new, superior, and more sophisticated way of doing things. The Spaniards looted and pillaged South America as well. The Indian subcontinent was not spared from British dominance and exploitation during a period of more than three hundred years.

Before the British occupied India, and the French large areas of Africa, we know that the Arabs had their own share of occupying lands, making the people of these lands their subjects, and exploiting them. Many people know about the transatlantic slave trade, but very little is said about the Trans-

Saharan slave trade that was put in place by the Arabs. The Africans that were taken across the Sahara Desert to the Middle East ended up working under deplorable conditions. Some of them were castrated to become eunuchs, who served their kings.

Africa, India, South America, and all the other countries that were occupied in recent history are not the first to experience conquest. Human history is filled with examples of conquest, occupation, enslavement, and dominance of one group of people over the other. Any attempt to try and use today's understanding to judge the past, without placing everything within the context of past circumstances, is doing a disservice and will be causing more harm than good.

We are looking at the past so that we can understand the lingering feeling of superiority that some have, while others feel that they are inferior because of the misinformation that has been fed to them for a long time. Again, this visit to the past is not intended for analysis paralysis or to play the blame game. We have already established that no one is good, and all have the propensity for taking advantage of others when the conditions are ripe. This is not an attempt to minimize or downplay the ills of the past either, because it affected real people and we are still experiencing some of the consequences today. That said, this book is about hope and the way forward. If we keep looking at what is behind us, we will miss what is before us and we will never get out of the present sense of hurt and hopelessness.

We look at the past so that we can have a better grasp of what is happening right now. Some of the legacies of the past superiority complex are still being manifested today.

You have been created by God, and the Bible, which is God's word, is the handbook that contains the instructions on what to feed your mind with. It also has information on what you are made of, and what The Designer had in mind when you were created. Therefore, you must and should listen to it and no other. Whatever society says or thinks will not override what God has said about you. You are wonderfully and fearfully made.

What you believe about yourself is what people sense when they meet you. As such, you must feed your mind with the right information about you. It does not matter what the government says, or what the society says, because you are not what other people define you to be, even if it is written in textbooks and broadcasted over TV and the radio. People's opinion about you should never be allowed to become your reality. You must refuse it and replace it with what your Creator says about you. Period.

Therefore, instead of trying to change the racist, focus on changing your belief system. For racism to work, it needs two kinds of people: those who, out of ignorance, believe and act as if they are superior, and those who believe that they are inferior because they have been told they are.

By the way, waiting for other people to accept you, before you accept yourself, is relinquishing the power of having the final say into the hands of others. It is a terrible idea to wait for the approval of others before you become comfortable in your own skin. You must lead the way by finding yourself and being happy for who you are, and not wait for others to give you their approval to be who you are. Resist the pressure from society and social media that wants to define who you are. They will never get it.

Chapter 4: Racism in the Workplace

Racism is very prevalent in our society and it is not uncommon to discover a news story dealing with urban revolts or police blunders attributed to racism. What is racism and what can we do to combat it? Try to learn more about racism and its effects at work, for example, how to react when you witness discrimination or when you hear about race or racism in the media.

If a teacher or your boss treats you differently because of your race or makes derogatory comments, it can be difficult to know how to react, because this person is in a position of power and has influence over your grades or your salary.

If you think this is unintentional behavior or simply the result of some form of awkwardness, and that you have a good working relationship with this person, you can talk about it together. He may not be aware of the extent of his behavior. For example, a teacher who consistently asks you to give your opinion as a black person, may not realize that it is hurtful, and that not all black people think the same.

If you talk to the person, do it privately when they have time for you. Talk to them about your feelings in a clear, direct and purposeful way. Explain that his behavior hurts you, you feel directly affected by some of his words or his actions, and you hope that it never happens again.

If you suspect that this behavior is intentionally malicious and you fear to discuss it with him for fear of reprisals (on your relationship or your working conditions), you must speak to his superior. It can be the principal in your school or the human resources manager of your company. Make sure you have documented your grievances. Schedule a private meeting to explain what it is you are reporting (including the frequency and quotes from the incidents you are reporting), and why it is not acceptable.

If you are the victim of racism at work or in public, you have recourses at your disposal. French laws protect you, for example, against racial discrimination.

Contact a lawyer specializing in civil or labor law if the racism of which you are a victim of, deprives you of housing, work, your security, or your individual freedoms. You will sometimes have to follow a very specific procedure to report these acts of racism, and a lawyer can assist you in your efforts and advise you on the procedures to follow.

If you want to file a complaint, but do not want to pay a lawyer, there are many organizations that can support you in this process (especially those specializing in human rights). Find out how to find the resources you need to speak out against racism.

Try to tell the difference between a person and a racist act. Racist people are full of prejudice and will rarely change, even if you confront them with their actions. Racist behavior, however, is sometimes unintentional and results from a latent culture of racism in our society.

If the person is racist, there is often no point in trying to make them change their mind or denounce their actions as racist. Your efforts will often be in vain and a waste of time and energy. They will certainly accuse you of being paranoid, or they may try to take advantage of your origins. It is rare for a racist to change their behavior just because it hurts you. It can also be dangerous for your personal safety to face these people.

However, if this is an unusual comment and you have no reason to doubt the goodness of the person in question, you can try to show that person how their words may be hurtful. People are sometimes oblivious to their racist acts and the effects they can have.

You can decide whether you will try to change these people as well as the racist laws or not. Nothing obliges you to educate them on this subject only because you are part of a minority.

Being a regular victim of racism can be traumatic for its victims. Know the people you can trust and rely on, to be more resilient when dealing with a racist in the future.

The stress of racism can affect your life, physical and mental health, academic performance, and can also expose you to serious illnesses.

You can join organizations, political parties, or other racial groups to meet people facing the same barriers. You can also talk with your family members and rely on them after a traumatic episode. Studies have shown that being able to share these negative experiences with people who understand you can relieve the stress that results from it.

Racism or racial discrimination on the job can be observed when the behavior of the company is altered based on race or ethnicity. Thus, staff encounter or observe it in various forms such as abuse, indirect and direct discrimination, or victimization. Research suggests racism is growing tremendously, with nearly a third of all employees experiencing racism in their distinctive jobs.

Prejudice or racial discrimination in the work environment can also be seen when the organization's conduct is modified based on race or ethnicity. It is hence experienced or seen by representatives in various structures, for example, badgering, aberrant and direct segregation, or exploitation. Research demonstrates that bigotry is also expanding, with nearly one-third of workers encountering prejudice in their occupations.

Identify recognizable variables that show the presence of prejudice in the working environment.

Experiencing Hostility in the Workplace

An antagonistic vibe can, for the most part, be experienced through verbal insults. For example, a dark-skinned American lady can be condemned for being forceful; a Muslim individual can be ridiculed for not drinking liquor during get-togethers; or an Indian might be ridiculed for their pronunciation. Hence, it is important for the managers inside an organization to be exceptionally aware of these key perspectives and avoid them. Frequently defrauded people in the working environment can be dependent upon allegations of being strange. Subsequently, people encountering bigotry will experience issues in associating with different individuals from the firm or getting along in a group because of antagonistic vibes. In the workplace, victimized people can often be accused of being out-of-place. Consequently, people experiencing prejudice appear to have problems in socializing with other members of the company or getting along because of animosity in terms of working as a team.

Overcritical Aspects of Racism

This type of prejudice is experienced when the directors are out-of-line in censuring the staff. For instance, the boss groups specific individuals of a similar culture. It is a method of rehearsing racial segregation at the work environment, particularly those dependent on their presentation. It can altogether demotivate the employees from working since they may lose trust in their capacity to deal with their jobs.

Importance of The Elimination of Racism in the Workplace

It builds multi-culturalism and coordination. It very well may be accomplished by making a domain that encourages the workers to feel they have a place in society.

It creates a terrible exposure for the organization. In addition to morals reasons, it is imperative to battle bigotry to construct a mainstream picture. Further, prejudice at work sits around and is managed at court hearings.

This creates a multiculturalist and integrative society. It can be achieved by creating an environment that allows the employees to feel that they fully belong to society.

It eliminates the company's bad publicity. Apart from ethical reasons, fighting racism is important to building a popular image. Therefore, when coping with court trials prejudice at work is wasting time and money.

In addition, racism in the work environment is indispensably influencing an enormous number of representatives and constraining their capacity to partake in the working environment. This is significant for the government, general public, the organization and the board, since it creates jobs to battle prejudice in the work environment.

Concept and the Theory Behind Different Approaches

Employment policies are generally accepted as fair if there are equal opportunities for all. What does fair chance mean, however? It ensures that decisions regarding jobs—for example, transfers, promotions, or selection of special training programs—will be based on merit alone. It ensures that considerations such as race, ethnicity or nationality will be insignificant, and will not be considered when deciding on work merit. In the recruitment and hiring of applicants, only criteria such as credentials, job skills and relevant experience will be used. It guarantees the equal treatment of all job applicants, and thus supports the principle of equality.

Convention 111 on Discrimination in Employment and Occupation, of International Labor Organisation 1958 (ILO) affirms that equal rights are paramount. The definition of discrimination is that it has the effect of annulling or degrading equal treatment or equal opportunities at work, on grounds of race, color, sex, faith, political opinions, nationality or social origin.

Discrimination can be directly or indirectly the core form of racism. There is direct discrimination when the employer refuses an individual employment due to his race, color or origin. It is a matter of intent. It is easy to determine the ability of the employer to recruit members of a certain class, whether indirect or implicated. Nevertheless, the purpose can also be inferred from the employer's behavior. Such an inference could be drawn if an employee fails to hire a qualified person from a particular race, and the position remains open to the same applicants from another race. These actions would be direct discrimination, unless the employer can explain the action on legitimate grounds.

Discrimination can also be indirect if corporate policies or activities systematically exclude employment opportunities for members of certain classes. Perhaps the most prevalent form of discrimination and the toughest way to eliminate it is that. This occurs when seemingly neutral job conditions systematically exclude people of a certain racial or ethnic heritage. These conditions include limits on height, weight, diplomas, and specific qualifications not relevant to the particular job. In its prominent ruling on *Griggs v. Duke Power Co. 1* in 1971, the Supreme Court of the United States ruled such discrimination unconstitutional. The employer wanted a high school diploma and an intelligence rating for jobs, that theoretically did not require such credentials. Although the employer may not want to discriminate, the court found that the conduct was unconstitutional, since it excluded black applicants, who otherwise qualified for the job.

Continuing consequences of discrimination, legal recourse against discrimination was intended to reaffirm and enforce the concept of equal opportunity. Indirect discrimination is held unfairly even if it is not proven accidental. Yet, there is a significant exception for the concept of equal opportunity. The current consequences of previous discriminatory policies are not considered. For example, barriers that exclude black people from certain jobs were an essential component of the system in South Africa during the Apartheid regime. Although apartheid is illegal in South Africa, today black people still suffer the effects of past practices of racism. For example, in South Africa today, when black people compete in terms of jobs, they are at a disadvantage because they do not always have the training they need since they could not get it under apartheid. They may also lack formal qualifications, since educational opportunities have been refused in the past. Even if employers are qualified, the employers may deny them on the grounds that, qualifications from organizations they have been familiar with or have previously hired, have not been achieved. Similar problems are faced by indigenous peoples in Latin America and elsewhere. We have been discriminated against for so long that we cannot compete in the same way, as those who have gained in the past.

The strict implementation of the equality principle does not take into account the historical factors, which are now a disadvantage for members of certain classes. The only consideration is to guarantee a position, promotion or other gain for the best qualified candidate. Equal opportunities are fixed in this case. This considers credentials of applicants only as they are, on the day the decision of employment is made, but does not investigate the impact of discriminatory policies on those who compete for jobs in the labor market. Nevertheless, given that cultures are not static, labor market fairness will not be achieved without considering the existing effects of past discrimination practices. Nonetheless, there are strong arguments to caution against this path and they should be considered carefully.

Equal treatment and equal outcomes occur when a system of equal opportunity ensures equal treatment and not equal results.

In this process, all participants are assumed to have the same basic means of achieving the desired goal, but not everyone can accomplish it. This is only achieved by the better qualified, for not all participants have the same skills. Equal chance is thus compatible with the concept of a market system, in which unequal outcomes are regarded as the engine for competition. Since the competition is an ongoing process for an optimal market system, those who fail to achieve their goal today know they will always have a new opportunity.

A rational reasoning for unequal outcomes is difficult to explain when inequalities arising from a historical pattern of racial discrimination are not clarified. Why do black people, or other minority groups or economically weak groups, not seem capable of catching up with economically or socially dominant group members? In the US, for example, race and ethnic minority groups tend to be underrepresented in high unemployment, despite huge efforts to achieve equality of opportunity partially, because members of groups which have been subjected in the past to racial discrimination will not compete in the labor force today. The unequal distribution of economic means also stems from the unequal distribution of goods in previous rounds of distribution.

This leads to the development of a vicious discrimination circle. The unbalanced outcomes are the product of yesterday's unequal results and will become a factor in tomorrow's determination of unequal results. How can this violent circle be broken then?

One solution would be to inspire discrimination survivors to work a little harder to improve their skills, and thus to be able to compete better for jobs. This approach has certainly brought remarkable results for some survivors of racial discrimination, but these are exceptional cases. Evidence indicates that the attempts of individual members of ethnic or racial minorities to resolve job limitations are often futile in communities where historical patterns of discrimination exist.

In the United States, for instance, black students are unemployed more than white people are, and black workers often fail to achieve promotions or improve their skills. There is evidence that when older black people improve their skills, they continue to decrease rather than raise their wages.

Stereotyping and Discrimination

Stereotypes are one of the reasons why racism exists, and why it is so difficult for survivors to resolve job obstacles through individual efforts.

The most familiar and disturbing example of stereotyping in the workplace is when equally qualified people compete for the same job, and there is only one difference: one belongs to a minority ethnic group. Because of stereotypes and other characteristics, employers usually hesitate to nominate a member of the minority group in these circumstances. The suggestion that they are lazy, dishonest, psychotic, addicted or abusive involves these stereotypes. With gender discrimination, the

European Court has recently acknowledged that stereotyping may have unconstitutional consequences in the field of employment and, therefore, strict measures to prevent stereotyping are justified. Decisions of employment based on such stereotypes reinforce and perpetuate the existing patterns of discrimination. Stereotyping is insidious, as those who rely on it often do not know their own biases. Stereotyping as a factor in decision making in jobs also goes against the view of some economists that the independent market forces will end discrimination. This financial understanding of racism should be carefully considered, as it is very important and quite persuasive on the surface.

Organizational management must watch out for examples of stereotyping, to which it can provide a basis for racial discrimination. Essentially, stereotyping is negative because it presents divisive generalizations, and applies them to all of the company's staff members and therefore can cause confusion. For example, individuals should be vigilant of the vocabulary used, and when other members or the management make derogatory remarks regarding specific elements of the culture and customs of an individual.

The point is that discrimination exists in the labor market, because businessmen who feel discriminated against cannot recognize the cost of refusing to work with people with whom they do not want to associate. Discriminating is expensive, and employers will not do so even where there are poor market conditions. Therefore, companies can only engage in discrimination if market failure occurs. In addition, companies practicing discrimination will quickly be removed from the market when free competition occurs, as their production cost will rise because they have to increase the pay of members of the ruling race or ethnic group in order to meet their demands for discrimination. The political assumptions behind this principle are that the most effective way to eliminate discrimination is market liberalization. This would put an end to racism on the part of the labor market and remove the profit motive.

It is abundantly evident that market forces also help to promote equal treatment and can help remove the most visible forms of discrimination. Nevertheless, the evidence available shows that discrimination in the field of employment is widespread even under open competition. The reasons for this are linked to stereotyping. The expectations of employers about the relative performance of workmen do not rely on objective criteria, but rather on subjective judgments based on dominant assumptions. According to Kenneth Arrow, racism exists. If employers find white workers to have more trust, productivity and hard work than their minority colleagues, employers would hire more white workers, thus reproducing existing racist patterns. The only logical way to break the vicious circle of racism is that employers be required to take proactive steps to ensure that it is eliminated promptly and effectively.

Development and Racial Discrimination

This section examines how, in developing countries, political, legal and economic conditions differ significantly from those of those in those countries, in which these institutions and strategies have their roots. The institutional framework and strategies outlined in the previous section may be successfully applied. This problem can seem meaningless on the surface. After all, the most developed countries have in recent years implemented regulatory frameworks inspired by models based on the experience of industrialized countries. Why should they not apply in the area of racism and employment?

It is widely accepted that policies against discrimination are more likely to be successful, if those responsible for designing them are aware of and rely on the best international practices. The quest for inspiration is obviously not the same as copying systems from other countries without any critique. It is necessary to determine needs in a realistic way, to ensure that organizations and services are tailored to local context. The relatively strong institutions, the effect of widespread poverty and unemployment and the effects of globalization on states' ability to regulate employment practice should definitely be considered.

The institutional issue of racism is both a social and a political problem, and an effective policy against discrimination will allow states and non-state institutions, such as syndicates and business associations, to be organized and coordinated. This strategy assumes that state institutions are prepared to engage with racial or ethnic minority members. This approach also includes a political regime open to competition and involvement. This strategy also includes a government, that believes that some responsibility for the enforcement of anti-discrimination laws can be delegated to an independent agency. Ultimately, the establishment of an independent judiciary is necessary, as it is the sole responsibility of courts to ensure that anti-discrimination policies are implemented under the constitution and law. The fact that anti-discrimination laws are widely seen as incompatible with the fundamental principle of fair rights is, therefore, important in an independent judicial system. The courts shall ensure that the interests of all people–both minority members and majority groups–are adequately protected.

It is difficult to satisfy these requirements. In developing countries, this is especially the case, with weak institutions and a poor democratic process. Nevertheless, ethnic intolerance and discrimination are often the key factors in some of these countries, that explain the fragility of the democratic process and institutions. We, thus, tend to have a vicious circle: flawed and poor state systems underpin discrimination, and shortcomings of racism seem inevitable.

Nevertheless, it can still break this vicious circle. This is illustrated by the experiences of South Africa and Namibia. Both nations, which had suffered under apartheid for many years, have, through democratic means, succeeded in introducing and enforcing robust anti-discrimination employment policies, that lead to an increase in the status of racially oppressed groups in the labor market in the past.

Both experiences can fairly be considered special, since the formerly marginalized group now dominates power in both countries. We do, however, have valuable lessons, the most important of which is undoubtedly that, the war against discrimination will not be isolated from the democratic process. It must be recalled that most racial and ethnic groups which are discriminated against are often usually excluded and are not entitled to the full exercise of their rights as citizens. Therefore, it is critical that the political system is opened in tandem with the elimination of barriers to jobs, and other public goods so that the victims of discrimination are properly represented and heard. This strategy will not only improve the democratic process but will also ensure that measures to eliminate racism are sustainable.

How to Eradicate Racism in the Workplace

Effectively Enlist and Recruit A Racially and Ethnically Diverse Staff.

While it is insufficient just to hire your staff as a 'rainbow' of individuals from various backgrounds, picking from an assortment of groups is important to begin with. Contact minority associations, social groups, systems, media, and spots, where individuals of various ethnic and social backgrounds assemble; to get the data. If you use informal exchange as an enlistment instrument, spread the news to individuals from those backgrounds or contact key individuals. Additionally, consider composing an equal opportunity strategy for recruiting and promoting staff.

Effectively Select Socially and Ethnically Assorted Board Members, Officials, and Managers.

Racial partiality can be decreased if the staff is diverse, and raises the consciousness of one another, yet racism is diminished when power is shared by the administration.

To move past racial bias and guarantee comprehensiveness, your association's board individuals and officials ought to mirror the communities or the voting demographic it serves. For example, one gathering chose to save a specific number of openings on its administering board for delegates of the social and ethnic gatherings in the community.

Converse with the ethnic minorities on your staff and ask them what hindrances or mentalities they face at work. Analyze your bulletin or different distributions, and fight against the negative depictions, rejections, or stereotypes.

Discover how you can improve your working environment for individuals from different racial and ethnic backgrounds that work there. This will not just give you the tools regarding what you have to change, it will likewise mean that the necessities of each group are paid attention to. Take a look at the works of art that you have in your workplace. Are any social events portrayed in a cliché way? Is there an acceptable diversity in the individuals depicted? For instance, if all the individuals in the prospectus flyer are European Americans, you should change that and showcase a more diverse team of individuals.

Structuring a group or driving a collection of trustees concentrated on shaping and checking an arrangement, for impelling circuit and fighting inclination in your working environment.

Racial tendency is decreased by making affiliations and guaranteeing that materials are socially delicate; yet predisposition is lessened when there is a gathering that winds up being a touch of the association structure to guarantee comprehensive and fundamentally institutional approaches.

Chapter 5: Why Is It Important to Eradicate Racism?

Here are some more reasons why racial discrimination and racism ought to be diminished:

- They hinder or keep the object of racism from accomplishing their maximum capacity as a person.

- They hinder or keep the object of racism from making their fullest commitment to society.

- They obstruct or forestall the individual or group taking part in racist activities, from profiting by the potential commitments of their casualty, and therefore, debilitate the network all in all.

How Media Can Eradicate Racism

Write letters to the editor of your local newspaper, or contact your local television and radio broadcast station, when the coverage is biased or when there is no coverage at all.

Contact the Local Media and Organize Presentations and Awareness Programs

You can organize seminars or webinars for staff, educating them about the values and traditions of diverse groups, and help them understand the negative implications of their coverage related to race and ethnicity.

How Neighborhood Can Eradicate Racism

Welcome all newcomers. Make 'Safe Zone' signs or stickers. Distinguish and change arrangements that are privileged and keep up the current state of affairs.

How Community Can Eradicate Racism

Arrange a cleanup or modifying effort to eradicate racist spray painting or take out vandalism. Set up 'Hate-Free Zone' signs in the community.

Organize a conference of community leaders made up of representatives from the different cultural and ethnic groups, as well as different community sectors (e.g., police, schools, businesses, local government, etc.), to examine their existing policies that support racism in any way and determine what needs to change.

Allow residents to discuss how racism influences your locale. This can give you an understanding into how individuals feel regarding the matter, and thoughts on what you and others can do to battle racism. It is an opportunity to let individuals who share comparable worries to connect with one another, and to openly tell racists that your locale will not represent racism.

Make a purposeful system that draws in neighborhood government, business, practice, media, and different pioneers to show your duty to kill racism in the organizations in your locale.

Uniting pioneers to make a procedure that intentionally, deliberately, and expressly manages racism will empower your locale to have a more extended term vision, for a fair and solid network. Every institution should discover a path for how to wipe out racism in its arrangements and practices. The media ought to be included to help get the word out. Trustworthy pioneers need to take an open remain to advance and approve the exertion. Work to guarantee that decent variety is esteemed and remembered for the regional government's statement of purpose

Put forth an attempt to help occasions that praise the customs of various social and ethnic gatherings.

This can be as basic as remembering such occasions for the network schedule and effectively publicizing them. Your association can likewise co-support these occasions to show its help.

Compose vigils, hostile to racism exhibitions, fights, or rallies.

When a racist gathering happens in your locale, sorting out a vigil, exhibition or open dissent will not just give you and others some viable method to react, it can additionally assist with planning your locale by having everybody come.

How Media Can Help Individuals Eradicate Racism: Fighting Racial Racism

You do not need to shape a gathering to take care of racism. As a person, there are numerous ways that you can take use to diminish someone else's bias, including:

- Cause a pledge to donate to when you hear racial slurs or comments that signal racial partiality.

- Exploit occasions and other instructive materials during Black history month or Hispanic heritage month and make it a point to discover some new information about various societies.

- Consider approaches to improve your working environment to advance racial understanding and value. Be proactive about making recommendations.

If you are a parent, give your youngster opportunities to go to occasions about different societies. Incorporate various conventions about child rearing and youngsters' celebrations into your parent instructor affiliation and your kid's school. Work with the instructors to organize such chances.

Changing individuals' perspectives and institutional practices is hard but essential work. A responsibility among people, associations, and institutions to esteeming decent variety is fundamental for solid networks. Changes will not occur without any forethought, yet you can start to make little changes towards having any kind of effect, as proposed in this chapter. These little advances construct the establishment for progressively sorted out, further, and bigger endeavors to manufacture comprehensive networks, a subject that will be talked about in the following part of this book.

Chapter 6: What Deepens the Racism Divide

If the races are so equal, why do racial disparities exist in so many areas? "It is racism," is the short and easy answer, offered by both knee-jerk liberals and conservatives throughout the world. It has become an article of faith; an unquestioned and unquestionable mantra.

Economic and academic racial disparities in America have become bootstrapped by conventional wisdom into serving as proof of pernicious white racism. Notice that this conclusion absolutely requires the assumption that all races are identically capable.

Black people suffer from crime, poverty and illiteracy much more than white folk. White people are predominantly in charge of American society (except, if one views Jews as being a race apart from white people, precisely as the Jews think of themselves). Therefore, white people must be responsible. Thus, goes the logic.

As we have seen, that is wrong. Otherwise, athletics would be a lily-white affair at all levels, whereas the reality is exactly opposite.

Why does racism seem to be so unevenly applied, if conventional wisdom holds true? Why do Asians do so well academically and economically, though the virulent white supremacist sneers at them with a contempt, equal to that held for all other non-white races? No explanation other than white racism is allowed, else we are drawn inevitably to the doorstep of admitting that racial differences exist.

Politically Correct Racism

Why is it so hard for the politically correct to admit seeing the obvious racial differences? Is it because they believe such differences necessarily create racial pecking orders, whereby some races are inherently inferior to others? If so, and this seems the only logical reason, then just who are the real racists around here?

Consider the last paragraph carefully. In fact, go back and read it again.

How ironic. The very people who decry racism are those who readily acknowledge the existence of racial differences, yet actually are the ones possessed of illogical racial attitudes. They are the real racists.

This is a vitally important concept that deserves to be restated. The politically correct refuse to acknowledge racial differences because they believe that such differences would be proof of racial inferiority. They refuse to see differences as being merely different. Theirs is a singularly racist outlook because of the negative implication they insist upon applying to racial differences. Those who deny racial differences have painted themselves into a corner. If ever they accede to the overwhelming proof of racial differences, then they immediately become the very racists about whom they complain so loudly. That is why they are stuck and unable to accept the overwhelming proof of racial differences, though their position so clearly is lost. However, the politically correct show they know the real score by the manner in which they handicap races they consider to be superior with such devices as affirmative action, quotas, profiling and diversity programs.

Golfers play with handicaps so as to make their routine game more competitive. Golf handicaps readily acknowledges the ability of some players to play the game better than others. Handicaps makes games like golf more competitive and, therefore, more enjoyable. Handicaps in life are unfair for those held back, while the less deserving take their places in line. For those far back in the line, the result can be a death sentence.

The Rationale for Affirmative Action

As Title VII, the Civil Rights Act was forced through Congress, just like with so many other pieces of ideologically driven legislation, notably the immigration bill that was to follow shortly thereafter, America was deceived. It was none other than Hubert Humphrey that told his colleagues in the Senate, "Title VII does not require an employer to achieve any sort of racial balance in his work force by giving preferential treatment to any individual or group." However, when the courts saw that black folk were not qualifying for jobs in the numbers approaching those suggested by their relative percentage of the population, they began to require that the number of black people hired be increased. It began in the public sector, as do so many unfortunate social ideologies, but quickly escalated.

Legacy of Resentment

Imagine that you are talented, black and truly deserving of all that has come your way in life. How can you ever know whether your achievements were born of merit or skin color?

Imagine yourself a black doctor, every bit as talented as white doctors on staff with you at the hospital at which you practice medicine. Now imagine the rage you feel when both black and white people express a preference for the same race doctor, because of their unstated belief that you could not have earned your position and therefore are not qualified to attend to their needs.

Now imagine yourself untalented and black, knowing that you do not deserve that which has come your way in life, yet resenting having it handed to you in so patronizing a fashion. Can the resentment of the undeserving somehow be denied the same gravity as that possessed by the unrecognized but deserving?

The racism of the politically correct now has become institutionalized throughout America, such that blacks are never expected to comport themselves properly, learn adequately or compete.

There are no teachers and no students in America today who are unaware of the intellectual disparity between white and black (and, to a slightly lesser degree, Mexican) students, save only those yet to occupy mixed classrooms.

Now schools are desegregating, a result that both black people and white people desire. Yet, America does nothing to address the real problems with black educational shortfalls, just as it does nothing to deal with the real problems of black underachievement in all areas of life.

We do not demand that black people actually do the homework that white people regularly turn in. We do not demand that blacks achieve test scores which show that material has been learned and retained. How demeaning it must be for black people in today's society, which refuses to expect excellence in minority performance, a refusal born of a very real racist belief in the inherent inferiority of blacks. A belief held by the very people who claim to be concerned for black interests.

The resentment is not confined to black people. Imagine being white and coming to a hospital emergency room, only to find that your attending physician is black. You do not know if he is qualified to operate on your badly injured child, yet they refuse your request for another doctor. Your child's life hangs in the balance. What will you do?

Imagine your resentment if your son just missed out on a spot in the freshman class of medical school, because several less academically qualified minority students were admitted.

Many black folks, both talented and untalented, are awakening to the legacy of affirmative action and they do not like it.

Some black people today speak of the creation, in a single generation, of an entire subculture that will not stand on its own, so crippled by handouts has it become.

Placed together with their intellectual equals, black people would likely thrive. Instead, society does its best to make as many black people as possible taste the bitterness of personal failure. The long-term consequences of such a strategy can only be negative, likely in staggering measure, for all races.

This was foreseen by Booker T. Washington, founder of the *Tuskegee Institute*. He said, "No greater injury can be done to any youth than to let him feel that because he belongs to this or that race, he will be advanced, regardless of his own merit or efforts."

The news gets worse. Members of the American entitlement subculture, largely black, but constantly swelling with large numbers of illegal immigrants, see nothing wrong with their own ever-increasing entitlement mentality, so immersed in it have they become. These people, too, resent white America for complaining about getting that which they have come to view as their own.

Meanwhile, resentment on the part of white people grows daily, as well as resentment of the racial preferences of the growing black resentment. The explosion in black-on-white crime, despite being covered up by America's government and media, serves only to aggravate the growing hatred on both sides.

Spread of The Entitlement Mentality

The entitlement mentality is not restricted to those already in America, either. When President Bush announced his Guest Worker Program, the flood across America's southern border swelled to tidal wave levels, comprised of those who literally (and indignantly, when caught by the US Border Patrol) said, "I am here for my amnesty." Their demands were made in Spanish, of course.

In a very real sense, we have created an entitlement mentality throughout the world by our actions. Is it any wonder that we face the same animosity everywhere that we have fostered in America with our misguided attempts at legislating equality?

Deepening the Divide

Some black people and a great many white folk realize that affirmative action and its progeny have created a deeper divide in American culture than ever existed previously, even during periods of slavery. This time, the divide is marked by silent seething and ever-growing resentment.

The media/government coverup serves only to aggravate things. Making white people feel guilty for their inherent racism (and if you do not think that guilt breeds contempt, then you quite simply do not understand the concept). Making black folk believe that white racism is at the basis of all black problems.

More Resentment on Both Sides.

Those who have little (black people in this case) always believe that society's output should be divided equally among everybody. Those who have much (white people) always believe in division according to merit. This fundamental and unrecognized schism exists in America today, and grows larger by the day.

There will be a race war, the initial skirmishes of which already are being fought in America's streets, that will bring an altogether new meaning to the concepts of race war and genocide, courtesy of those who claim to abhor racism. The irony would be amusing if the situation were not so deadly.

At the highest levels of golf, such as in open tournament play, handicaps are removed. The same is true for the ruling elite, of course. The rules, the handicaps, apply to everybody but themselves. Of course, they can afford to live apart and above the rest, can they not? They can afford to escape the consequences of their very real racism and pretend that, because they do not deal with the issue personally, they are not racists. For now.

This living apart by the elite must not be confused with "white flight" from cities to the suburbs and the rural districts of other states altogether. White people in general are depicted as the aggressors in the black/white racial war that is erupting from the cities of America. However, aggressors do not retreat, do not forget. White people simply are seeking the safety that they once found together in cities.

Chapter 7: How to Subdue and Eliminate the Racist in You

An everyday example shows how this is possible. For example, nobody was born with the ability to drive, and yet by the time many individuals become adults, they find themselves not even thinking about it even as they expertly maneuver the car. Someday, with regular practice, egalitarianism could be like driving a vehicle: a skill acquired over time, but in time, so automatic as to be second nature.

So, what are some techniques that you could utilize in stopping the racist in you? There are a lot, of course, but below are six to bring into consideration that follow from the scientific insights we describe.

Consciously Commit Yourself to Egalitarianism

However, recognize that oblivious bias is no more the 'genuine' you than your cognizant qualities. You are both the conscious and the unconscious.

Recognize Differences; Instead of Images That You Are Disregarding Them

Become friends with individuals from various groups, so as to build your mind's nature with various individuals and extend your perspective.

It is normal to concentrate on how individuals are not quite the same as you. However, attempt to intentionally recognize what characteristics and objectives you may share for all intents and purposes.

When you experience instances of unambiguous prejudice, take a stand in opposition to them. Why? Because that makes and strengthens a standard for yourself and the individuals around you, notwithstanding giving some assistance to the individuals who are the objectives of implicit and explicit partiality.

Those are steps you can take at this moment, without waiting /thinking that the world will change.

Yet, this examination has suggestions that work out in a good way past the personal. The brief instant response of a cop who shoots an unarmed black man, probably will not be totally different from your own. Rather than posing the question of whether an individual is or is not supremacist—since each of us is a mix—we can start thinking about the manners by which we may build our social condition to address prejudice and its most exceedingly terrible impacts, without accepting that anyone stage will be a sweeping fix.

Realizing that prejudice is a piece of the structure of our psyches we can ask, for instance, how might we change policing with the goal that the aftereffects of predisposition are less deadly? How might we address the monetary imbalance between various gatherings to diminish the weight on networks that are verifiably the objectives of bigotry? What can school areas do to ensure tutors come in positive contact with various types of individuals, and prepare them with steps that help them intentionally lessen unconscious prejudice inclination?

There are numerous fronts in the crusade against racism, both certain and unequivocal; yet they all have one thing in common: us. We are all conceivably part of the issue—and we are all able to turn into a piece of the solution.

Chapter 8: Racism in The Society

Real Estate and Racism

Think of prejudice. Do your contemplation, go to Klansmen waving crosses around or signs that state boldly, "NO BLACK PEOPLE, NO DOGS, NO IRISH." It is anything but difficult to target separation when it so self-evident. Notwithstanding racial guiding and the distinctions in the treatment of individuals of various races or societies, things get cloudy.

One of the realtors' (many) tasks is to maintain the Fair Housing Act, (42 U.S.C. 3601 et seq.) which implies that we are not permitted to control individuals towards the "proper neighborhood for individuals, uh, similar to you folks". We are not permitted to decline to show homes to individuals since they have committed the transgression of having a skin that is a couple of shades darker than our own. Or then again lighter. Or then again whatever.

In any case, it appears that even today, we are still slipping in the squalid ooze of bigotry. Easily overlooked details, similar to that joke your manager made yesterday, or the supporting inquiries of your most recent customer about the "blend" of an area, or then again, the notorious "I'm not a bigot, yet... [insert bigot remark here]". The issue with neglecting things like, "I'm not a bigot, but..." is that it doesn't change anything.

What we, as realtors, and as individual inhabitants of the planet Earth, need to do is stand up and state, "No. No, it is not alright for you to do/not do/express those things."

How would we go about it? Indeed, there is consistently the virus gaze and the cold, "I ask your acquittal." There is the, "that is hostile, and I would prefer not to hear it, or anything like it once more." There is even, "I'm sorry you feel that way. It does not seem as though this business relationship is going to work out."

On the web, there is constant talk on blog entries that feel this has gone too far. There are detailing individuals in informal communities who target others. There are your own blog and site, where you can clarify your position.

The virtual world of sites, web journals, and so forth are a hotbed of explanations that criticize individuals of a particular race or ethnic birthplace.

Put your assessment out there and challenge individuals who offer expressions that put individuals down as a result of their race. Remember that your customers may get their work done on the web - would you like to be viewed as supporting bigotry with your silence or challenging it?

It goes past making the best decision. Keep in mind, you are securing yourself as well. Bigotry harms everyone, regardless of whether they are an individual from the targeted race or not. In the event that it is alright to direct a Chinese individual away from a specific apartment suite. At that point, it is alright to do something very similar to a lady, a Jew, a redhead, an individual more than 65 years old, a family with youngsters. A similarly biased, oblivious thinking can be utilized to reject pretty much anyone from the fundamental privileges of homeownership.

As realtors, we should be progressively mindful of these unobtrusive prohibitions and be set up to confront them head-on. It has been said online that, "there is a bad situation for bigotry inland." I oppose this idea. There is an entirely agreeable spot for it in our profession. Our main responsibility is to make that spot vanish.

Chapter 9: How to Change Your Mentality on Racism

Turning out to be hostile to racism begins with changing your own outlook, these specialists said. This implies, for instance, that when you have a partial or racist thought, you hold that idea and reconsider it before acting it out.

Dislodging partiality in your brain can be hard on the grounds that it is normally an oblivious inclination, Tatum said. You cannot sift through inclinations except if you are mindful of them.

Tatum compared generalization presentation to taking in brown haze noticeable all around: "They are so inescapable in our condition that we are continually breathing them in. What is more, as an outcome of breathing them in, we ought not be astounded that occasionally we inhale that out."

Address the issue by asking yourself what you are spilling into the air, regardless of whether it is generalizations or oppressive conduct. Mindfulness is the initial step.

It is an ideal opportunity to begin finding out about race. Tatum's book can clarify why dark-skinned understudies discover alleviation in hanging out together in the midst of all the bigotry with school.

Find Out About Microaggressions

Some white individuals realize that to become hostile to bigots, they should begin to tune in and look over the historical backdrop of prejudice in their nations.

A few people are clearly portraying racism conduct as a glimpse of something larger, calling individuals bigot names or undermining individuals based on race. At that point there is the piece of the ice shelf that is not effectively noticeable to individuals, in the event that they are not looking. This incorporates a scope of unobtrusive yet treacherous mentalities, practices and approaches.

Microaggressions can be deliberate, unexpected or even good natured, yet they impart threatening, critical or negative racial suppositions to the recipient. Furthermore, they insidiously affect a colored individual's mind and proceeding with racism suppositions.

These bigot inclinations are clear to the ethnic minority. However, they are so instilled in the non-non-white individual that they are accepted to be socially worthy.

Subduing A Racist Mindset

Being against racism implies more than freeing yourself of bigot mentalities, convictions and practices. It implies you are additionally effectively battling that indefensible trinity, as it shows throughout your life regularly.

Giving to lobbyist associations and fighting shameful acts are unquestionably acceptable beginnings, to turning into an ally. In any case, that is insufficient. Effectively refuting partialities in your own circles is vital to enduring change, as those thoughts and convictions—except if tested—are what our youngsters assimilate and are woven into the texture of our way of life.

What that implies for you, relies upon what your identity is, the place you live and who you are communicating with.

Everybody has specific effective reaches, in which we can help shape the mentalities, and along these lines the practices, of others. Ask yourself what messages you are sending to your family, companions, work environment, spots of love and outside exercises. What authority would you say you are giving, or would you say you are quietly supporting prejudice?

Individuals once in a while think, 'Well, I'm not calling anybody names, or doing anything scornful, so I have no duty." In any case, the arrangement of this web forces us all into silence. So, you need to oppose it in the areas where you are.

Chapter 10: How Racism Affects the Victim's Mental Health

Bigotry is the consequence of the intrusion of the foolish thought of the crude side of the human soul into the human inner voice of the individuals, who despise colored individuals. Whatever is foolish and merciless in human conduct has its starting point in the foolishness of the counter, small voice, which is our wild, fierce, corrupt, and remorseless inner voice.

People of color are as insightful as white individuals. Bigotry is unadulterated madness and must be dealt with like every psychological maladjustment. This should be possible through dream treatment since the oblivious brain that creates our fantasies works like a psychotherapist. All fantasy pictures contain valuable messages, that fix the human brain of the ridiculousness forced by the counter inner voice.

Mankind's history is set apart by savagery. Different boorish weapons, torments, wars, and numerous annihilations, incited by fear-based oppression, demonstrate that humankind is fundamentally unreasonable and savage.

We are perilous primates with a little human inner voice. This is the reason our discouraged populace cannot discover harmony and satisfaction. Hate is a horrendous toxin that wrecks the human heart. It likewise decimates the whole world with its hurtful incitation.

Prejudice is savagery and mercilessness against the individuals who have brown complexion simply because the supremacist becomes blockheaded when the counter inner voice controls his conduct. The individuals who show hatred against another person, simply because of the shade of their skin, cannot be viewed as silly.

Hate against anybody is the aftereffect of the mastery of the small voice into the human inner voice. There is nothing human in the small voice's tendency. It is a wild creature that can think, however, has no affectability. Its realism is crazy, and it does not regard moral standards. The person turns into a genuine beast when he is ruled by his crude nature.

The barbarity against people of color, during the period of the Brazilian colonization by the Portuguese, gives us the most stunning demonstration of human madness. The barbarity of bigoted associations, like the Ku-Klux-Klan in the United States, is another stunning proof of the profundity of human evil.

Despite the fact that bigotry is today denounced by numerous individuals, and the dark-skinned populace figured out how to accomplish better social positions, remorselessness and twistedness against people of color is still a stunning truth. Africans live in neediness. The same happens to their relatives, living in different nations of the world.

Until today, the preference against dark-skinned individuals forced them to confront different fears. They do not have indistinguishable open doors as the white populace, and they are not rewarded in a similar regard.

In any case, dark-skinned individuals are exceptionally skilled, and their languishing over such a large number of years is absolutely out of line. The bigoted mentality is uncivilized and strange. We should put an authoritative end to bigotry on Earth.

This marvel will happen when everybody will dispose of the harmful impact of their enemy of heart; when wildness and gloom will quit portraying our development; and when everybody will be delicate and humble. Only shrewdness and sympathy can totally dispose of savagery and craziness.

Addressing Black Racism

There are a number of people of color in America who detest white individuals - every single white individual - and consider them to be racists. This mentality is uninformed and dishonest and it ought to be discarded altogether.

During the last few years, a ton was done in America to battle bigotry. It was disgraced in the public arena, media and the scholarly world, and projects were established to assist dark-skinned people to succeed. While in other nations, bigotry proceeds in unrefined structures, in the most recent decade and a half, black people have progressed admirably. Africa is developing; and many people of color have gotten exceptionally persuasive in world undertakings. America had a dark-skinned president, and African authority has, generally, improved. Dark-skinned individuals accomplish much. The less of them slaughter and plunder their own, the more they turn against genuine racists, and the more powerful the individuals of all extractions who need bigotry gone become. This turns into a significantly more suitable, and a considerably more legitimate way than assaulting white individuals for being white individuals. The better the direct of one's kin, the better their notoriety, the more grounded the body of evidence against bigotry and the less persuading the contentions of those white people who are racists no doubt.

The occasions of the most recent decade have demonstrated that people of color can achieve whatever white individuals can achieve. This implies their consideration ought to be coordinated toward such achievements. The more these individuals accomplish, the less persuading will be the contentions of genuine racists. Also, that will do unquestionably more for people of color than any measure of dark-skinned bigotry or scorn toward white people for being white people.

Excellence Is Your Best Weapon for Fighting Racism

To build up the weapon of greatness, we should make the most of all the instructive open doors that are accessible to us. Despite the fact that the entryways of chance are not generally opened similarly to everybody, there are still approaches to be what you need to be, go where you need to go, and have what you need to have. Also, it does not make a difference where you live, or how poor you are. You, despite everything, can succeed. For whatever length of time that you have your wellbeing and can think, achievement is conceivable.

Tolerating the way that the entryways of chance are not open similarly to everybody, one thing that is equivalent for everybody is time. There is a similar number of hours in the day for us all. How you utilize these hours is your decision. You can utilize them on the play area, or you can utilize them to play the books. Playing on the play area may allow you a few hours of quick happiness yet playing the books will give you long haul delight.

African Americans and different minorities can no longer utilize the fact of being poor or living in an awful neighborhood or humble community to shield us from accomplishing greatness through training. Sometimes, the more unfortunate you are the more instructive open doors there are accessible to you. Neediness ought not be a reason for not working up to your latent capacity. Regardless of how poor you think you are, there is consistently somebody who is less fortunate.

Kindly do not be humiliated by or embarrassed about the size of your old neighborhood. Numerous people from modest communities have gotten extremely fruitful and ascended to the highest point of their callings. That recipe is difficult work, commitment, assurance, and a modest quantity of entertainment. Like any great formula, a few fixings are a higher priority than others. In the event that you are making a cake, you utilize significantly more sugar than salt. What is more, if you need to have cake, difficult work ought to be your sugar and entertainment your salt.

For those African Americans and different minorities who are going to mostly white schools, you should utilize the logical way to deal with critical thinking. At the point when researchers and architects tackle issues, they generally state what is given and what is accepted. It very well may be given that a specific educator or instructor is supremacist, or you can expect that the individual in question is a bigot. In any case, you should discover an answer for the issue. I am not pushing in the homeroom, yet you ought to pick the correct weapon for the correct event. For this situation, making "an" in the course is the best weapon.

In the event that you think prejudice is awful now, simply envision how things were thirty years prior. Allow me to repeat, you ought not to let prejudice or some other sort of "-isms" shield you from being effective. Frequently you will hear some minority understudies at chiefly white schools offer the expression, "if this spot were not all that bigoted, I would improve in school." Our country is misguided of being effective, in light of the fact that all prejudice will never be expelled from our schools or society. The probability of this occurrence is about equal to discovering elephants perching in trees. You ought to reconcile that when you are teaching the field to progress, you will hit a couple of rocks. A portion of the stones will be dark skinned, some will be white, and others will be all hues in the middle. Whether or not the stones are dark-skinned or white, on the off chance that you need to cut a decent gather, you would be wise to continue furrowing. It is the seed you disperse that chooses what your gather will resemble. You cannot plant corn and hope to reap tomatoes.

The shading problem brings about inner persecution. Inside, mistreatment can lay lethargic until other life injuries happen. People who become mindful of their disguised persecution can utilize passionate treatments to help them to unwind social messages that may have added to individual injury and confidence.

Chapter 11: Let us Join Hands and End Racism

The intention of this book was not to dwell on the negativity associated with racism, ethnocentrism, and tribalism. Care was taken to demonstrate that a social construct such as racism has no place in any civilized society, but it has persisted because society continues to give life to it. In this final chapter of the book, I am going to hammer the last nail on the coffin in which racism is to be placed and bury it.

Here are some of the things that will put an end to racism, once and for all. All of these are going to be focusing on what you can do to change you. If your focus is changing other people, you are going to get frustrated, discouraged, and will give up.

Know Who You Are

When you know who you truly are, nobody is going to mess with your mind. I have shown that racism is a social construct based on a faulty ideology about people's identity. According to the racist, there are some people whose skin color makes them inferior to them and deserving to be treated as such.

However, it is not enough for somebody to believe that your skin color or anything else makes you inferior to them. To be inferior, you need to believe that you are inferior. As simple as this may sound, many have stumbled over this basic and foundational idea that all are created equal because some have a hard time believing that they are not superior, and others will not shake off the idea that they are <u>not</u> inferior.

You are a child of God. In addition to being created in the image and likeness of God, you become a child of God when you recognize that the fellowship between you and God needs to be reestablished. You become born of God when you believe in the name of Jesus Christ. For it is written:

You Have the Final Say

The ball is in your court! You have the power to kick it towards any direction you choose. This book is about you as an individual, not about the government, institution or organization. I mentioned that the governments, laws, and organizations are the other players in this issue, but the main thrust of this book has been YOU. There is no point in chasing the wind because you will never be able to catch it. I say this to underscore the important fact that you should stop focusing on those that believe to be superior because they are not. Stop believing those who believe that you are inferior and treat you as if you are.

The power is in your hands, because when you refuse to believe what other people say about you, it will render it useless.

This book is not only for those that feel that they are inferior; it is for those that believe that they are superior. It may be shocking to hear that you are not superior, but whoever told you that you are superior to others lied to your face. It is time for you to come down from your high horse and face the reality that "all men are created in the image of God." Therefore, you should stop being part of the problem and start being the solution by treating all people with respect, honor, and dignity. You are not going to lose anything if you treat other people right. When everybody is empowered to reach their full potential, you, too, will benefit.

Stop using skin color to classify and treat people. There is, has been, and always will be one human race. This may be a hard truth to swallow, but it is the truth that will set both the oppressed and the oppressor free. Anybody that accepts this truth, believes, and acts on it, can boldly and confidently ask, "racism, where is thy sting?" The good news is that there is no sting, because we are all equally created in the image and likeness of God. There are no children of a lesser God!

Conclusion

Trying to change an ignorant and bigoted person is not your job. This book has thoroughly explained racism and the dimensions of racism in the existing world, and how it faces both a benign and malignant neglect in the criminal justice system, not just in America but all across the globe. How white supremacy has subjected the black people and browns in white majority countries to sheer discrimination and indifference, has also been explained. Not just that, racism has deep roots in the medical and health sector as well. Black people and people of ethnic minorities are cornered when they suffer from any disease that incites a judgmental sentiment in the society, whereas the privileged class always gets away in such situations much easier.

Racism is not reversible. Social or cultural experiments in which the dominant production of difference is simply reversed, may be instructive to understand the mechanisms of racist marking. However, they remain individual attempts and will not assert themselves as a collective racist knowledge, because they lack the necessary structural and institutional anchoring. For this reason, racism also no individual prejudice or personal opinion, but expresses social relations and the social power relations inherent in them.

Racism will not express itself independently of social power structures, because it is always dependent on a reinforcing space: the unity of knowledge and institution. In equality-oriented societies, racism is difficult to discuss because it is seen as unjust and illegitimate.

The call of this book is "let us join hands and fight racism in our countries."

www.ingramcontent.com/pod-product-compliance
Lightning Source LLC
Chambersburg PA
CBHW071235020426
42333CB00015B/1490